7 FUNDAMENTAL RIGHTS OF CITIZENS OF GOD'S KINGDOM GOVERNMENT

. . . .

ANDREW DARRAH

Ark House Press
arkhousepress.com

© 2022 Andrew Darrah

Scripture quotations from The Authorized (King James) Version. Rights in the Authorized Version in the United Kingdom are vested in the Crown. Reproduced by permission of the Crown's patentee, Cambridge University Press

Cataloguing in Publication Data:
Title: 7 Fundamental Rights of Citizens of God's Kingdom Government
ISBN: 978-0-6454117-2-0 (pbk)
Subjects: Salvation; Christian Living;
Other Authors/Contributors: Darrah, Andrew

Design by initiateagency.com

Please permit me to start with definition of the words which make up the title.

The word **fundamental** describes something that forms a *necessary base* or core or something of central importance. Other words such as *root, primary, key, essential, basic, principle* and *original* are all words that can be used in place of the word fundamental.

In this context, the word **Rights**, describes that which is always right to do or to have according to the Right-giver, the Creator God.

Kingdom is the territory ruled by the King, the Creator God.

Government is authority exercised by the King over everyday behaviour of citizens of His Kingdom.

As in any government, a citizen of God's Kingdom government has rights and responsibilities or duties. As I stated before, a right is that which is always right to do or have. A **right** is a privilege, and that means you may choose to make a claim on it or not. A **duty, however** is that which is required of the citizen.

Below is a list of seven rights, three of which are also duties in God's Kingdom Government. Whatever was made available to man from the beginning in the book of Genesis forms the basis of these rights.

1. The right to hear and the duty to obey the Word of God.

2. The right to life, health and wholeness.

3. The right and duty to participate in the rulership of the earth.

4. The right and duty to work

5. The right to freely eat

6. The right to marry and have as many children as can be raised to the Lord.

7. The right to rest, or to be at rest.

In most instances, your life is preserved through access to these fundamental rights. You are able to live freely and become all you were created to be. It is therefore important to understand that your basic human rights can only come from your Creator as He is the only One who has the ultimate goal, and the sole responsibility to preserve or sustain the life of His creature.

That brings us into a very important truth.
Your fundamental rights as a human does
not, and should never come from another
human. No human has the authority to
determine that, simply because all humans
are equal. Only God, the Creator is the
prime determinant of the basic rights of all
humans.

Now let's go to the very first, the **Human
Right to hear and duty to obey the Word
of God.**

*The Lord Jesus stated in the book of
Matthew chapter 4 verse 4, that man shall*

*not live by bread alone but by every word
that proceeds from the mouth of God.*

The scripture above highlights the truth
that the life of humans depend on hearing
and obeying *every* Word of our Creator.
That implies that to hear and obey God
is to live, but to refuse to hear and obey
God is to die or lose the life that comes
from Him. In the book of Genesis, after the
Lord God created Adam, He gave Adam an
instruction to eat from every in the garden
except of the tree of the knowledge of good
and evil. Obedience to the instruction by
Adam meant life, but disobedience meant
death as the Lord added " the day you eat

of the tree, you shall surely die." So you see right from the very beginning this principle was established, hearing and obeying the Creator is life, and disobeying the Word of the Creator is death to the creature.

Because your life depends on it, It is your God-given right as a human to hear His Word and your duty to obey Him. The implication is that, nothing or no person or group has authority to keep you from accessing, hearing and obeying the Words of your Creator. Remember that your very life depends on it.

In the book of Matthew chapter 28 verse 18, The King Jesus charged all citizens of His Kingdom (we know them as disciples or followers) the common task of preaching the gospel. He adds in the verse 20, "Teaching them to observe whatsoever I have commanded you." The basic right to access or hear the Word of the Creator also puts you in a place of duty to obey the Lord's Word at all cost. Even if that means being persecuted or killed. The Lord Jesus assured His disciples or citizens of His Kingdom that those who lose their life for His sake will find it (ref Mathew 10:39). Blessed are those who are persecuted for righteousness sake, for theirs is the Kingdom of Heaven (ref Matthew 5:10). **Once again you have**

the right to hear and the duty to obey
***EVERY* Word of your Creator, the Lord**
God. His Word is life to those who find
them, and health to all their flesh (ref
Proverbs 4:22)

That brings us to the **2nd Human Right** in
God's Kingdom Government. The right to
Life, Health and Wholeness. This right
is the direct result of hearing and obeying
His Word. As we have seen in the book of
Genesis, Life was the result of obedience.
As long as Adam and Eve remained obedi-
ent to the Lord, life, health and wholeness
were theirs. No sin, and therefore no sick-
ness or diseases. They were wholesome.

That was their fundamental right, and no one, not even satan could take that from them apart from getting them disobey the Lord God. Thus the Lord God revealed His intention for His creature. Man was to be full of life, healthy and whole from the onset. Like all of God's creation, man was good until he lost His rights through disobedience.

The Lord Jesus who came to fulfil the law, and to empower His people to obey God also declared that He came that we might have abundant life (ref John 10:10). As you commit to pursue and obey the Word of the Lord, the Word produces life in you.

The Word is Spirit and the source of life
(ref John 6:63).

The book of Acts chapter 10 and verse 38
records that the Lord was anointed with
power, and went about doing good and
healing all that were oppressed of the devil.
"...Himself took our infirmities, and bare
our sicknesses (ref 2 Pet 2:24). It is NOT
the Will of the Lord, and therefore against
your basic right in the Kingdom of God to
be denied the rights to the full life the Lord
gives you due to diseases in the form of
bodily ailments or mental disorders, or any
form of oppression by satan. That is why
Lord Jesus in His earthly ministry commit-

ted Himself to heal the broken-hearted, to preach deliverance to the captives, recovering of the sight to the blind, and to set at liberty them that are bruised (ref Luke 4:18). It is the **Will of your Creator, and therefore your basic right is to be full of His life, be healthy, and whole as you remain obedient to Him.**

Choosing to disobey God's word thereby living in sin keeps us from this right. The wages of sin is death...(Rom 6:23). We see many examples in the scriptures where sin was tied to sickness or some form of torment. In some instances, a **citizen of God's Kingdom must confess and repent from**

**any known sin, in order to lay claim on
their right to life, health and wholeness
(see James 5:16).** Remember that obeying
the Lord leads to life, but disobeying the
Lord results in death.

The whole of God's commandments to
man is summed up in love for God, which
is to live in obedience to His every word,
and love for people. Walk in the royal law
of love, which is also known as the law of
liberty (ref James 1:25).

The **3rd Human Right** in the God's Kingdom
Government is to **Rule the earth. "Let
us make man in our image and likeness**

and them have dominion (ref Gen 1:26)."
That was an instruction to all men in the
image and likeness of God, authorised by
the Creator to contribute to the management or rulership of the earth. It is the
right and duty of every disciple of Christ
to partake of the rulership of the earth
and to determine the course of the world.
This is further emphasised in the book of
Matthew chapter 28 verse 18, where the
Lord assures His disciples that He has all
authority, both in heaven and earth, and
therefore commissions them to go and
disciple the nations. As we can see, some
of our God-given rights also puts us in a
place of duty.

The born-again, saint, child of God, citizen of the Lord's Kingdom, and disciple of Christ cannot just sit back, watch and complain about the state of the world. He/she must rise up, claim their right of rulership, and get involved in the state of affairs by living and preaching the gospel of the God's Kingdom. The gospel has the power to save and change lives. It is greatest instigator to change in the world.

The more lives are changed through the power of the gospel, the better things will get in the world. "But how can they believe on Jesus whom they have not heard, and how will they hear without a preacher..?"

(ref Romans 10:14). The Lord has therefore given every one of His children the right and privilege to shape the course of this world simply by living out, preaching and teaching the gospel of God's Kingdom Government to the lost people of the world.

Through the scriptures, we see that the Lord has always looked to His people to restore sanity to the earth. In the Book of Psalms 82, the Lord commands His children to defend the poor and the Fatherless, the Lord judges that the earth is out of course because His children have failed to administer justice on earth.

The United Nations have their own anti –
God agenda for the earth. Every child of
God, and a member of the body of Christ,
must align with, and propagate God's
agenda for the earth. The prayers and deeds
of the saints should be thy kingdom come,
thy Will be done on earth as it is in heaven.
"Let them have dominion or rulership over
all the earth". That is your God-given fundamental right and duty.

The **4ᵗʰ and 5ᵗʰ Right** in God's Kingdom
Government is the right and duty to **work,
and the right to Freely Eat.** To work is to
offer some type of service in exchange for
a wage. Like all the other rights, the prece-

dence for work is from the very beginning. " The Lord God formed the man from the dust of earth and put him in the garden to dress and keep the garden, and then made for him a helper, his wife, Eve. The right to work is linked to the right to rule. The goal of rulership is to produce and maintain order, and order requires work. Whether the work is the management of a garden like Adam and Eve, or directly providing some type of service to people, the underlying principle is that every true work brings some sort of order to the earth.

Here are some general guiding principles around work that we can learn from the book of Genesis chapter 2

- The Lord decided the type of work for the man.(see verse 15)
- Because the work was given by the Lord, the wage also came from the Lord. "You are free to eat from any tree in the garden" (see verse 16)

In the New Covenant, the Lord God has a vacancy, an open invitation to every one of His children to join in the kingdom work of reaching the lost for Christ. The Lord is building His Kingdom on earth, and is after labourers or workers who would prioritise the preaching and teaching of the gospel of the Kingdom, and promote the kingdom lifestyle to draw souls into His Kingdom. The Lord says the workers of the Kingdom are paid good wages. He put it in the following words, John 4 verse 34 and 35 "My food is to do the Will of Him who sent Me, and to accomplish His WORK. Do you not say, "There are yet four months, and then comes the harvest'? Behold, I say to you, lift up your eyes and look on the fields, that they are white for harvest. **Already he who reaps is receiving wages and is gathering fruit for life eternal;...**

On occasions where the Lord sent out his disciples to go and preach the gospel of the Kingdom of God, He also told them to take nothing with them. The precedence can be derived from Matthew 6 verse 33, if you seek first the Kingdom of God and His righteousness, what you will eat, drink and wear is added to you. That is a great assurance, that as long as we prioritise the work of Lord's Kingdom in our various endeavours of work, having a mentality, not to necessarily work for income, but focus on reaching out to souls for the Kingdom, the Lord becomes your boss and pays you. "The wages are good, He says."

There are challenging times ahead as we approach the end of all things. The apostle John prophecies in the book of Revelations chapter 13 verse 16 and 17, a time of economic difficulty, where people of all classes will not be able to participate in the economy unless they receive a mark which is a sign of worship of satan. It is important for the saints or children of God to understand that their source of provision is ultimately from the Lord as they live a life committed to the work of the Lord's kingdom.

Remember, one of the main reasons why you were created is to work. Therefore work is your God-given right and is backed up by

His Authority. That means that as a child of God, you do not need to panic about economic fluctuations. Simply seek the Lord on what He would have you do for work, and regardless of the type of work, make it about the Lord's business. Let the Lord be your ultimate boss in your line of work, your wages will come from Him.

Kingdom minded saints or children of God will always have their needs met regardless of what happens. For the Lord says a worker (being a worker of the Kingdom) is worthy of his pay. You have a fundamental right to work, and to freely eat as you seek first the Kingdom of God and His righteousness. Your daily bread comes from the

Lord. "Today give us our daily bread" (ref
Matthew 6:11).

The 6th Human Right in the God's
Kingdom Government is the right to
marry and have children. The institution
of marriage is also from the very beginning.
It was God's idea. God joined the man and
the woman, commanded and blessed them
to multiply and fill the earth. Fill the earth
with more humans after the image and the
likeness of God.

The family is the Lord God's mechanism
to expand His Kingdom Government over
all the earth. He intended marriage and

family for His own eternal purposes. For that reason marriage and family is always to be under the Lord God's jurisdiction. The apostle Paul under the inspiration of the Holy Spirit wrote in the book of 1 Corinthians 7 verse 28 that it is neither sin nor against the will of God to marry. In the book of Malachi chapter 2 verse 16, the Lord expresses His hatred for divorce, not only because it is the breaking of the covenant of marriage but also beacuse it destroys families, and thereby hinders the Lord's purpose of having godly children out of godly marriages.

As a child of God and citizen of His Kingdom, the governments of this world does not have jurisdiction over your marriage and family. The events of this world should not dictate whether you marry or not, or have children or not. Getting married and having as many children as you are able to properly instruct them in the ways of the Lord is your God-given right.

The 7th Human Right in the God's Kingdom Government is the right to **rest.** In Genesis 2:2-3, we read that the Lord God ended His Work on the seventh day. He rested on that day, therefore blessed it and sanctified it. In Mark 2:27, the Lord

Jesus said that the sabbath was made for man. We have already established that one of the main reasons God made man was to work (ref Genesis 2:15). When we connect the above scriptures we see that the Lord God intended for man to work for six days and rest in one, just as the Lord God Himself did.

The book of Hebrews however presents a broader scope of what it means to rest beyond physical rest from work. We are admonished to enter into God's rest in order to cease from our own works. The "rest" referred to here which is beyond physical rest from work. It is the rest one experiences or should experience when one gets born-again, and become a citizen of God's Kingdom Government. The God-given human rights denied to them at the fall of man is restored. They are once again given full access to their rights in God's Kingdom Government.

The full access and restoration of these rights brings them into this "rest" of God. For they which have believed do enter into rest. (ref Hebrew 4:3). In the Kingdom of God, righteousness is not worked for, as in the law, righteousness is imputed as a free gift to those who submit to the Lord Jesus (ref Romans 5:17). Through the Holy Spirit we are able to walk out this free gift of righteousness, the fruit of which is peace and joy, a state of rest. Through the finished work of the Lord Jesus, we who believe are brought into this rest of God, and therefore cease from the works of self- righteousness. Full access to all these fundamental rights are granted by God's own righteousness freely imputed when one repents, believes in the finished work of Christ, baptise in water, and receives His Spirit with endowed power to live righteously.

EQUALITY OF ALL MEN

The book of Genesis Chapters 1 and 2 presents to us a guide as to what we can do, or not do, or have, and not have. These chapters clearly reveals God's will for man without question. For example, we know that all humans are equal because God's instruction to rule the earth was to all humans. That instruction, and right was not given to a privileged few people. Adam and His wife Eve were representing all subsequent generations after them. God did not create, and never intended a higher class of humans who governed the rest. All men created in the image and likeness were given the common responsibility to govern, not other humans, but the fish of the sea, and the fowl of the air, the cattle, all the earth and every creeping thing that creeps on the earth (ref Gen 1:26). For this reason the Lord, through the scriptures has always expressed His anger against injustice and oppression of men by other men. His very Kingdom is founded on the principles of righteousness and justice.

In the book of Matthew, the Lord warns His disciples against lording it over people as the Gentiles, He explains that leadership in His Kingdom is to be a servant. The Lord Himself, being the Prime example. Equality for all men is the Lord's highest goal for man on earth, and He seeks to achieve by the establishment of His Kingdom Goverment on earth.

It is of great importance that you as a child of God, and a citizen of His Kingdom does not look to the governments of this world to claim these rights and fulfil your God-given duties. You make claim only from the One that gave you the rights in the first place and fulfil your duties to your King, the Lord Jesus. The point is, even when the governments of this world are in any way doing all they can to keep you from God-given rights and duties, you must ulti-mately take it up in petition to the Right-giver, He will see to it. Unlike the governments of this world, **the very foundation of the Lord's Kingdom is righteousness and justice.**

Righteousness and Justice are the foundation of your throne (Psalms 89:14)

To have access to all the rights that I have discussed according to John chapter 3 verse 3, you must first be BORN AGAIN, (REPENT and BELIEVE in the finished work of Jesus on the cross for the forgiveness of your sin, and then be BAPTISED IN WATER and RECEIVE THE HOLY SPIRIT to be empowered to live righteously).

www.ingramcontent.com/pod-product-compliance
Lightning Source LLC
Chambersburg PA
CBHW060102050426
42448CB00011B/2592